# ARE YOU READY?

# ARE YOU READY?

## HOW TO PREPARE FOR
## AN INTERVIEW & GET THE JOB

### STEPH CARTWRIGHT, CPRW

Published by Off The Clock Resumes, Nine Mile Falls, Washington.
www.offtheclockresumes.com

Printed in the United States of America.

ISBN: 1534956263
ISBN-13: 978-1534956261

# ABOUT THE AUTHOR

Steph Cartwright is a Certified Professional Resume Writer, LinkedIn Profile Specialist, and the Founder of Off The Clock Resumes. She started as a freelance writer and discovered her passion for helping job seekers secure new and better jobs.

Steph began her career after several years in office administration and customer service. As a moonlighting freelance writer, she was exposed to various styles of content writing only to fall in love with resume writing.

She launched Off The Clock Resumes, an online resume writing and social media optimization service, in 2014 and has personally assisted hundreds of job seekers achieve their career goals. With her sights on developing a brand to lead the next generation of resume writing, she's developed innovative personal branding services outside of traditional resume and cover letter writing.

# PREFACE

I am not an interview coach. I'm not even a Certified Career Coach. I don't claim to be an expert in interviewing, but I have participated in more than I can count. No, I didn't struggle to find work. In fact, my problem was never in landing a job.

My story starts in customer service. The retail industry is not for me. I transitioned into hospitality, another form of customer service, and I actually enjoyed the work. I loved being able to make someone's day. There were guests in all sorts of circumstances: visiting town for a business trip while missing his son's first birthday, arriving after a stressful flight across the country for the funeral of a niece who died tragically and far too young, and checking in after being told the previous hotel had overbooked and given away his room to name a few.

The hotel I worked at give us the flexibility to give room upgrades, gift free meals, and even order flower deliveries. It was rewarding working in hospitality. However, new management came in and several changes made it difficult to provide the hospitality that made working there so rewarding. I quickly landed another job at a law firm as an administrative clerk, but I found out quickly that working in the legal field was certainly not for me.

I started exploring the opportunities available for freelancing remotely. I got a few website content writing gigs, wrote a few blog posts, and even edited a nonfiction manuscript for a local professor.

I started resume writing by answering a Craigslist ad as a contractor and editing a few resumes for friends and colleagues. I had a few referrals too and discovered that my resumes were securing job interviews for my clients within days. I never thought my strengths in strategic writing would make a difference in the lives of others.

Nothing drives me more than hearing that a client has received a new and better job. I've been there. Like so many of my clients, I struggled to find that fulfilling role in the workforce. I've worked for horrible bosses, companies that just don't care about their employees, and startups that were doomed to fail from the start.

I am so fortunate to have discovered my passion and my purpose so early in life. I'm driven to help my clients achieve the same. So how does this tie into interview skills?

Interviewing, like resume writing, is mostly common sense. It's difficult for people to think from a perspective that is uncommon to them. For example, what do you think an employer is thinking within the first few seconds of looking at your resume? Would *you* call you for an interview?

Interview skills are derived from common sense. The person who will be interviewing you has a goal. This person is looking for certain things and rarely is this person looking for something that wasn't included in the job description.

The spirit of this book is to share some common sense in an easy-to-grasp format and challenge you to look at your background from a new perspective. If you have common sense, then there's no reason why you can't conquer your next job interview and get the job.

# TABLE OF CONTENTS

# CHAPTER 1

## INTERVIEWS EXPOSED

Interviews are necessary events during the hiring process. Interviews can be stressful for job seekers, but employers need a way to assess your qualifications and personality apart from your resume. Your resume gives a snapshot of your background with the intent of providing more detail in an interview. The interview is the opportunity to sell your personal attributes and your strengths in applying your credentials to solve problems in the workplace.

## SO WHAT ARE THEY LOOKING FOR?

There are two main things that employers are looking for during an interview. First, they are looking to see if you are a good fit for the company based on your qualifications. Secondly, they are looking for whether or not you are a good fit for the company culture.

There are several tactics hiring managers will use to narrow down qualified candidates and find the best fit for the position and company. The interview process may be as quick as a single traditional interview ending with a job offer.

The interview process could potentially involve several, if not all, of the following types of interviews before receiving a job offer.

*"First, they are looking to see if you are a good fit for the company based on your qualifications. Secondly, they are looking for whether or not you are a good fit for the company culture."*

## PHONE INTERVIEWS

One of the first phases of the interview process is a screening interview over the phone. Not every company will call you for a phone interview, but you should be prepared nonetheless.

The interviewer may ask you to schedule a phone interview or ask if you have time to answer a few questions at that time. Whether you schedule for another time or take the plunge, you'll want to be somewhat prepared.

Employers will use phone interviews to narrow down the candidates. The interviewer will ask questions related to your background, specifically your past employment, your previous compensation, why you are looking for a job or leaving your current employer, and your salary requirements. The interviewer may also ask questions about your interest in the company.

While you may be caught off guard by the phone interview, you can ask to reschedule for another time. Asking to reschedule will not disqualify you but it will give you a chance to research a little bit about the company more and be more prepared.

# VIDEO INTERVIEWS

In the modern job search, video interviews are growing more common. With free software like Skype, video interviews are viable options for companies to screen candidates if they are not local.

There are several logistics to manage before a video interview. You'll want to check the time zones to make sure you aren't late for your interview. You will want to verify who is responsible for placing the call and to have a backup plan if technical issues arise.

If you anticipate a video interview in your future, you should create a Skype account since it is still the industry standard for video software. Choose an appropriate and identifiable profile name, profile photo, and status. Make sure to test your mic, your camera, your light source, and your internet speed. You should also place a test call with a friend to smooth out any technical issues before it counts.

Unlike a phone interview, presentation matters. Dressing in clothes that would be appropriate for a traditional interview is essential. You will want to talk slowly and clearly to avoid the "like", "um", and "uh" speech. Remember to look at the camera rather than the screen as well.

*"Unlike a phone interview, presentation matters."*

You will want to eliminate all distractions wherever you plan to do your video interview. This includes roommates, family, pets, background noises like laundry machines, and programs on TV or your devices that may distract you. It's a great idea to keep your resume, cover letter, and job description in front of you for reference too.

## TRADITIONAL INTERVIEWS

Traditional interviews involve meeting one-on-one with a hiring manager ranging from 30 to 90 minutes. You will be asked a range of questions about you, your background, your strengths and weaknesses, your career goals, and what you know of the company and job opening itself.

The majority of this book will discuss traditional interviews. We will specifically discuss how you should present yourself to employers, how to answer the most common interview questions, and how to follow up after a successful interview.

## BEHAVIORAL INTERVIEWS

Behavioral interviews focus heavily on your experiences with past employers. The questions will be situational and require you to have specific answers prepared.

It's common for interviewers to ask behavioral questions at traditional interviews as well. The best way you can prepare for behavioral interviews is to spend time before your interview reflecting on your previous jobs. Identify a few memorable situations where you helped solve a problem.

The key to answering behavioral interviews is to take your time. When asked a question about how you handled a situation, briefly describe the problem. Describe how you solved the problem and what you learned from the situation.

Behavioral interviews can also require that you describe a solution to a hypothetical situation. Again, think about how you could apply your strengths and expertise and answer thoughtfully. These interviews are a great way to assess a candidate's confidence and competency.

# PANEL INTERVIEWS

Panel interviews, also known as group interviews, may involve meeting with several interviewers or interviewing along with other candidates at the same time. While panel interviews can be stressful, this is a great opportunity to stand out from other candidates.

When meeting with a panel of interviewers, you will be asked an array of questions ranging from common interview questions to behavioral interview questions. Rather than worrying about your answers, focus on making a connection with each interviewer.

When in a group interview with other candidates, the challenge is in making a connection with your interviewer and being memorable. The tendency may be to blend in, but showing off your personality and asking questions will help you to stand out.

*"When in a group interview with other candidates, the challenge is in making a connection with your interviewer and being memorable."*

# TESTING INTERVIEWS

On occasion and typically for a second or third interview, you may be asked to complete an assessment or exercise that will demonstrate your skills. A testing interview will challenge your problem solving skills, your technical knowledge, or possibly your communication skills.

If you are given a timed assessment, do your best to answer each question quickly to give yourself the opportunity to go back and check your work after finishing the assessment. Try to rely on your first instincts when completing the exercise. They are often right, but it's always smart to check your answers.

## APPRENTICE INTERVIEWS

Apprentice interviews are a great final step in the interviewing process. Apprentice interviews are also known as working interviews. During the working interview, you will be asked to watch and participate in daily tasks that will be required of you if you do land the job. The primary goal of this interview is to see how well you fit in with the company culture.

Apprentice interviews also assess how you handle pressure. It's essential to remain calm and take your time. It's much better to do things right than fast during a first impression. This is also a great time to ask questions and to ask for feedback. Show that you want to improve on your skills.

# CHAPTER 2

## WHY YOU SHOULDN'T WING IT

When I started looking for my first job, I didn't take interviewing seriously. Like most high school students, I was applying for jobs that didn't require skills. I also had spent enough time in school and doing homework that studying how to do well in an interview or practicing interview skills seemed tedious.

When I needed a job to live on my own and pay my own bills, I changed my perspective to some degree. Yes, my interview mattered; however, every interview I had up until that point ended with a job offer. I never struggled to get a job, so I didn't need to fix what wasn't broken. Right?

Your interview says so much about you as a person. How you present yourself is only one side of the equation. When you walk into an interview unprepared and with the mindset of, "Oh, I'll just wing it," you emit arrogance rather than confidence. You typically answer interview questions insincerely, and employers notice.

I know of professionals who apply for jobs and attend interviews for positions they are not actually interested in to freshen up their interview skills. While I think this practice is disrespectful of the time of the interviewer, I think the intentions are brilliant.

## START MARKETING YOURSELF

When you secure an interview, you have a great opportunity to market yourself to other professionals in your industry. Even if you know nothing about marketing, the concepts are also rooted in common sense.

Like a company, you are a brand that will either invoke a positive or negative reaction from the interviewer. Your brand is a reflection of how you present yourself, your attitude, your personality, and what makes you unique. Your resume has already advertised your strengths and value. Your interview is your sales meeting.

When you prepare for an interview, you are walking into a sales opportunity equipped with the tools you need to reach your goal. When you know the job description inside and out, the company's values and mission, and the department's needs, you have all you need to sell your strengths as the solution.

*"When you prepare for an interview, you are walking into a sales opportunity equipped with the tools you need to reach your goal."*

When you don't prepare for an interview, you show a lack of genuine interest in the company and the position. You show a lack of interest in your own career and goals. You also show a lack of respect for the time of the person interviewing you.

Walking into an interview with the intentions to market yourself as a solution, your chances of securing a job offer increase. It's very difficult to market yourself as a solution when you don't take the time to explore the needs of the company and assess how you can meet those needs.

## GET CONFIDENT

Preparing for an interview will require you to take a good look at yourself. How you perceive yourself may not be how others see you. Looking at yourself through the eyes of an employer can be tough.

What an employer considers an accomplishment or a major contribution may be insignificant to you. You can't rule it out though. I remember refreshing my resume after two years of professional resume writing. I had no idea that many of my insignificant tasks could be looked at as valuable experience and accomplishments to an employer.

For example, I worked at a hotel for 14 months. During that time, I never felt like I achieved anything. I was just there to give a smile and hand out room keys at the front desk. Toward the end of my employment, the front desk agents (myself included) were really struggling to keep up on all the different groups coming and going. We were given one binder to look through before our shift on a daily basis.

During a team meeting, we collaborated and decided that we would get a large white board and update it every week. I volunteered to update it every week and within a month we were doing phenomenally better at handling large groups. We were more informed on room rates and special requests, and our satisfaction rates were skyrocketing. I didn't consider it a major contribution worth bragging about until years later.

What made it a major contribution? I only volunteered, but it showed leadership skills. It was only a weekly task, but it showed organization and dedication. It wasn't even my idea, but I still contributed to streamlining a major aspect of our day-to-day activities and increasing our guest satisfaction.

Once you start evaluating your experiences and identifying your selling points, you'll start to gain a bit of confidence in your strengths and value. Use that confidence to your advantage.

## PRACTICE NEVER HURTS

Preparing for your interview should involve practicing with a friend or family member. Mock interviews help you think on your feet. The best way to practice, whether over the phone or in person, is to have a list of interview questions and have your friend ask the questions at random. Your mock interviewer should observe how you are presenting yourself and how well you are communicating.

Ask your friend to evaluate your attitude too. Are you showing enthusiasm? Are you giving genuine answers? Should you be making more eye contact? Are you coming across more arrogant than confident? These are all important aspects of how you present yourself.

*"Are you showing enthusiasm? Are you giving genuine answers? Should you be making more eye contact? Are you coming across more arrogant than confident? These are all important aspects of how you present yourself."*

Your mock interviewer should also help you craft your answers more thoroughly. If you are struggling to develop a sincere answer for your greatest weakness, your friend may help you identify something you could improve on.

## IMPROVE WITH FEEDBACK

Additionally, you should take previous feedback from interviewers seriously. If a previous interviewer commented on certain achievements, make sure these are addressed in your next interview. While every interviewer will be looking for different things, highlighting what you've already been recognized and praised for won't hurt you at all.

Get in the habit of asking for feedback after each interview. It's a bold move, but it helps you get better. Interviewing is no different than any other skill you may possess. You should always strive to improve your interview skills by applying the feedback you receive and making changes to the way you present yourself and communicate.

# CHAPTER 3

## YOUR PHONE INTERVIEW

The first step in narrowing down candidates for a job during the interview process is to screen candidates over the phone. Phone interviews typically last 15-30 minutes but can last longer depending on the interviewer. This is your first impression apart from your resume, and you will be one of up to 20 phone calls.

The interviewer is primarily calling to verify that you are qualified. You will be asked important questions about logistics and expectations related to the positon before diving into your experience. Most interviewers will call without notice and ask if you have time to answer a few questions. You can certainly ask to reschedule for another time, but try to keep it within that day if not within the next business day. Remember the interviewer will have several calls to make, and he or she will be looking to get through the process and hire someone as quickly as possible.

If you do decide to take the call and start the phone interview immediately, make sure you have a distraction-free place where you can talk. Since you may not have any notes or your resume in front of you, take your time to answer the questions, especially when asked about your background.

## HOW YOU CAN PREPARE

If you ask to reschedule your phone interview for later that day or the following day, you have a little time to prepare. Don't invest too much time researching the company or rehearsing interview questions. You may find out quickly that the job or company isn't a good fit. The interviewer may also decide that you aren't a good fit based on the preliminary questions asked too.

First, you will want to try to find the job description for the position you will be interviewing for. Get in the habit of printing or saving job descriptions to your computer or phone when you apply for a new opportunity. Don't rely on bookmarking as the company may remove the listing from the website at any time. You will want to use this to quickly review the responsibilities and requirements to help defend your qualifications.

You will also want to do some brief research on the company. Find out what they do and what their customers have to say about them. Does the company have a great reputation for customer service? Does the company support causes that you share a passion for?

## QUESTIONS ABOUT YOUR BACKGROUND

The phone call may start off with the interviewer asking you to "Tell a little about yourself." This question is not asking for your life's story or a direct reread of your resume.

Summarize your past employment and what your career goals are. You should also mention any major events, such as a recent engagement, or personal interests to humanize your background but keep it brief.

You will likely be asked to describe your last few jobs including the names of the companies, job titles, job descriptions, and dates of employment. You will also likely be asked why you are unemployed or looking to leave your current employer. Keep your answers positive. Don't speak negatively about an employer.

Depending on the interviewer, you may also be asked about specific challenges in your previous jobs and how you overcame them. While the interviewer will be looking for more detailed answers during a traditional or behavioral interview, you will want to provide adequate information to answer the question and present the value you offer.

## QUESTIONS ABOUT LOGISTICS

If you do not live close to the company, the interviewer will ask questions about your location and transportation. Depending on the job description, you may be asked if you are willing and able to travel. It's important to be honest about your willingness to commute or travel in their service. If you have any hesitations about relocating, traveling, or commuting, now is the time to say so and not after you are offered the job.

## QUESTIONS ABOUT YOUR EXPECTATIONS

The most common phone interview questions that can narrow down candidates quickly involve salary. You may be asked what your starting and ending salaries were at your previous jobs and what your salary expectations are moving forward.

You do not want to sell yourself short. If you are overqualified for the position and need to earn more than the company can offer, it is not a good fit. You do not want a job that gives you financial stress. There are circumstances where you may be able to take a pay cut. Explain those circumstances carefully.

*"You do not want to sell yourself short."*

For example, I had a client who was in his sixties and returning to the workforce after several years of retirement. Despite his 15+ years of management experience, he was looking for an entry-level customer service job to keep him busy during the day. In this situation, I highly recommended telling an interviewer that he loved working with customers and wanted a role where he could excel in customer service rather than supervising other employees.

I also recommended he tell the interviewer that he is open to opportunities for advancement but that he thrives in a service-oriented environment rather than sitting behind a desk. Doesn't that sound so much better than, "I'm bored with retirement and just want something to do during the day?" Employers would rather see your drive and passion than hire someone who is happy settling for something below his or her qualifications.

You will also be asked questions about your expectations of the job and company. What are your career goals? What are you looking for in your next job? What is your ideal work style or environment? These questions will determine whether you could be a good match for the company culture.

# CHAPTER 4

## WHAT TO RESEARCH AND PRACTICE

Once you conquer your phone interview and schedule an in-person interview, you will want to thoroughly prepare. You will be asked much more specific questions about your background, your strengths and weaknesses, and your career goals.

You may need to prepare for a traditional interview, a behavioral interview, a testing interview, or a combination. Your interview can last 30-90 minutes depending on the employer, so there will be much more to prepare for than the phone interview.

## WHAT THE COMPANY VALUES

Most companies have, at the very least, a basic website. Take a look at the company's About Us page and Mission or Values page. You may also be able to gather some basic information from the job description. Discover what the company values.

What are the skills and experience that they value? What type of employee are they trying to attract? This information will be very important when an interviewer asks what you know about the company or why you want to work for that company.

## WHO RUNS THE COMPANY

The website should also have some basic information about who runs the company and who the leadership team is. While you may not be asked about this information during an interview, you may learn something really exciting and worth asking about in the interview.

For example, the CEO may have recently received a humanitarian award for his or her contributions to the community. If being active in your community is important to you, you could mention in your interview how excited you were to see that Mr. "CEO" received an award for helping the community. This shows you did your homework and are taking a strong interest in the company.

If you are unable to find information about the company's leaders on their website, you may find them on LinkedIn. If they are publicly active on LinkedIn, you won't need to send connection requests to view their background information.

## NEWS & RECENT EVENTS ABOUT
## THE COMPANY

You should also check the company's News or Events page on their website. If the company just celebrated their 20th Year Anniversary or another landmark event, commenting on this during your interview will show genuine interest in the company's growth and activity. You could also ask questions about upcoming events, such as how this position plays a role with the event or if you should participate in the event.

You should also do a Google search or two to see if the company has been mentioned online for a significant reason. The company may have recently hosted a leadership conference or seminar. This would be something to bring up during the interview to express your enthusiasm for growing as a leader.

## WHAT IS IT LIKE TO WORK FOR THE COMPANY

This is a little harder to investigate. If the company has a social media presence, you should start with Facebook and Instagram to see behind-the-scene photos or updates on what's new in the office. If the company is older and more conservative, you may not even find an active and current Facebook page.

*"If the company has a social media presence, you should start with Facebook and Instagram to see behind-the-scene photos or updates on what's new in the office."*

Another great tool to use is LinkedIn. Use the search tool to find people who work at the company. Your results can be narrowed down by Job Title or Location. Once you find a couple of employees in the department you would be working for, you can reach out with a connection request.

Send a Personalized Invite, and ask if he or she would be willing to tell you about working for the company. Let him or her know that you have an upcoming interview and are interested in learning more about the company culture beforehand. If you choose the right people to ask, it may get back to the interviewer and further show your genuine interest in the company.

## WHAT THE COMPANY DOES

If you walk into the interview and can't tell the interviewer what the company itself does, you're going to be in trouble. Does the company provide a service or a product?

You should also find out who the company's ideal customer or client is. The company website should have a Services or Products page with information on what they provide for their ideal customer. Identifying who their ideal customer is may be more challenging. Look at what the company guarantees. Do they offer a quick turnaround? Do they offer a free trial? Do they continually run online promotions? These traits will help you identify who they serve.

## WHAT'S NEW IN THIS INDUSTRY

You should do a little research to see what is new in the industry as a whole, especially if the company is in a technical field. Technology is constantly changing and getting better. Knowing what is trending in the industry or in your specific field will help you stand out.

If you are changing careers or new to the industry completely, you will certainly want to learn as much as you can about industry trends or recent news to stand a chance against candidates with more years of experience or more substantial qualifications.

*"Knowing what is trending in the industry or in your specific field will help you stand out."*

You can start by searching for industry-related blogs. Many of the companies you are interested in may have blogs with industry-related news, so start there. Also expand your search to similar company websites or online magazines.

## WHAT IS EXPECTED IN THIS ROLE

You should not only study the job description that the company provides, but you should also do a little homework on similar job descriptions. For example, you may apply for a sales position that advertises that they want someone with great lead generation skills. Another company may identify that they want their sales professionals to have great cold calling skills. Even though cold calling wasn't listed on your job description, you should point out that you have experience in cold calling. Another candidate may not, and it may help you to stand out.

Don't just pay attention to the requirements section. Read through the company information provided to determine which attributes they are looking for as well. They may be looking for someone with a college degree, but they may be looking for someone with a solid record of dependability and may weigh that attribute higher than the education.

*" Don't just pay attention to the requirements section. Read through the company information provided to determine which attributes they are looking for as well."*

## WHO YOUR INTERVIEWER IS

If possible, find out who will be interviewing you by name. You can use LinkedIn to learn more about what that person values, what causes that person cares about, and how they identify their role within the company. If he or she has a completed profile, read through the Career Summary. This section should give you some insight into what aspects of the job may be important or even what kind of interviewer he or she may be.

No, this is not stalking. If you want to stand out, you have to do the work. Sending a Personalized Invitation to connect on LinkedIn that introduces yourself and expresses your excitement for the upcoming interview is a positive and professional way to get conversations started.

## WHAT TO PRACTICE

Once you've gathered a lot of information to work with, you should study your own resume and practice identifying examples in your work history and education to help answer questions. There are several lists online with the most common interview questions and answers to give you a great starting point. We will address several of them in the next chapter.

You will want to practice answering questions about your career goals. Your goals are a key piece to your personal brand. Having a 30-second elevator pitch that identifies the value you offer and your goals is a great way to stand out. You may be asked questions about how this job aligns with your career goals. You will want to have a confident answer prepared.

*"Your goals are a key piece to your personal brand. Having a 30-second elevator pitch that identifies the value you offer and your goals is a great way to stand out."*

Practice identifying examples of how you applied your strengths and skills to specific situations. If you claimed to have organizational skills on your resume, have examples to back it up. Make sure you can defend what you say on your resume.

# CHAPTER 5

## WHAT (NOT) TO WEAR

How you present yourself in an interview is a direct reflection of the value you offer. You will be a representative of the company, and your interviewer will be assessing whether you are the type of person the company will want based on qualifications and presentation.

Your resume did the work of expressing your qualifications. This interview will tell employers whether or not you can present yourself and an organization professionally.

### WHAT SHOULD YOU WEAR?

Dressing up is always better than dressing down. Unless the interviewer says otherwise, you should prepare to dress in business formal attire. If your interviewer doesn't specify right away when scheduling your interview, you should ask. It's a common question.

# BUSINESS FORMAL
# FOR MEN

Business formal attire for men includes a solid color suit or suit jacket with matching slacks, long-sleeved button-down shirt, a belt, a tie, and conservative shoes. Navy or dark grey suits are the most appropriate since a black suit may be too formal. Your long sleeve shirt should be coordinated with the suit or white. Your belt and shoes should also match, and you should be wearing no jewelry.

Since presentation is everything, you should have a conservative hairstyle and neatly trimmed nails. Having a briefcase or portfolio for your resume, references, or letters of recommendation may be necessary as well. Make sure you or someone you know will be able to tie your tie correctly so you are not scrambling and frantic an hour before your interview.

# BUSINESS FORMAL
# FOR WOMEN

Business formal attire for women may also include a suit or a suit skirt, professional blouse, conservative shoes, and a portfolio or briefcase. A conservative dress and suit jacket may also be appropriate for the interview. The suit can be black, navy, or dark grey. Your suit skirt should be long enough to be conservative while sitting, and neutral pantyhose may be necessary as well.

Limit your jewelry and makeup to present yourself professionally. Your nails should also be neat and clean. When planning for the shoes you will wear, make sure they are conservative and comfortable to walk in. You don't want to break in a new pair of heels during your interview.

## BUSINESS CASUAL
## FOR MEN

When an interview calls for business casual attire, men will want to wear khaki pants or slacks with a long-sleeved button-down shirt, polo shirt, or collared knit shirt. A sweater is also appropriate if the weather is cooler. Conservative shoes are still necessary, but you may not need to wear a tie.

Business casual attire never includes a casual t-shirt, jeans, sneakers, or sandals. While the work environment may be more casual, the impression you leave with your presentation is just as important.

*"While the work environment may be more casual, the impression you leave with your presentation is just as important."*

## BUSINESS CASUAL
## FOR WOMEN

Business casual attire for women will include a sweater or blouse and cardigan or jacket, slacks or khaki pants, conservative skirts or dresses, and conservative closed-toe shoes. Business casual doesn't vary too far from business formal, so you should keep your makeup and jewelry conservative and professional.

## STARTUP CASUAL

Startup casual is a new trend that involves a more relaxed environment and relaxed expectations. Startup casual permits cotton tops and skinny jeans compared to conservative shirts and blouses with slacks. Blazers with dark jeans are also acceptable.

## MORE TO CONSIDER

Aside from maintaining good personal hygiene, you should make sure your nails are short and clean and your hair should be neat.

Men, your facial hair should be groomed and intentional (no five o'clock shadow please). You should also have mints available for fresh breath.

Take a good look at your interview attire and check for any loose buttons, stray threads, excessive lint, or pet hair. You will also want to bring copies of your resume, references, and letters of recommendation in a portfolio or briefcase to keep them organized and clean.

While in your interview, you should not chew gum or keep sunglasses on your head or around the back of your neck. Remember, how you present yourself is a direct reflection of the value you offer.

# CHAPTER 6

## ANSWERS TO
## COMMON INTERVIEW QUESTIONS

There are thousands of websites with lists of common interview questions and how to best answer them. You are not going to be able to study and be prepared for every question you are asked. It's essential that you take your time to answer any question asked of you.

The most unexpected interview question I have ever been asked was, "If you were a fruit, what would you be and why?" I completely choked. I had prepared for hours the night before, but I never would have had a solid answer for this.

I was actually embarrassed that my friends and family came up with answers quicker than I could. Just in case you are asked, you could be a grape because you work well with a team. You could also be a banana because you are sweet but have a thick skin when it comes to handling stress.

## TELL ME ABOUT YOURSELF.

Employers already know you are qualified for the position. That's why they called you to schedule an interview. When they start off the interview with a broad question like this, interviewers are looking to see how well you will fit with the company culture and if your goals align with the goals of their ideal candidate.

Start off with your Branding Statement. If you don't have one, this question alone is a great reason to have one. A Branding Statement should identify your overall profession, what value you offer, who your ideal employer is, and what differentiates you from other candidates. The point of your Branding Statement is to briefly summarize you and your goals.

From there, add in a few personal details but keep it professional. If you are really passionate about volunteering for a certain charity, say so. Did you just finish your first marathon? Tell them about how well you did and if you're looking forward to your next. Hobbies and interests that show you are a healthy and productive individual will make a huge impact.

Topics to avoid would be any political or religious activities. While these activities may be very important to you, they could open the door for discrimination. Discussing controversial topics may jeopardize your chances if your beliefs and convictions don't align with the company's views. It may not be fair, but they're looking for a great fit in addition to a qualified candidate.

## WHY SHOULD WE HIRE YOU?

This isn't a trick question. It's a fair question to evaluate your confidence and how well you understand what the company is looking for in this role. Understanding the role and the company values is a huge advantage when answering this question.

Take inventory of your skills and accomplishments and how they relate to the job description. The items that overlap are certainly ones to identify. Then have a couple of solid examples from your background of how these strengths make you the best candidate for the job. When you can explain to the interviewer what the company or department's main pain points are and how you can solve these problems, you set yourself apart from other candidates.

## WHAT IS/ARE YOUR WEAKNESS(ES)?

This is not an opportunity to turn a weakness into a strength. In fact, this is one of the most overused and ineffective interviewing tactics. Interviewers don't expect you to be perfect, but they want to see how you plan to improve.

Identify something you struggled with in the past. Maybe you struggled with communication skills, time management, or sales tactics. Describe what actions you took to improve and express how you are always looking for opportunities for growth. For example, you improved your communication skills by taking a public speaking course at a local college. Another example is using a daily planner or similar app on your phone to improve your time management skills.

## WHAT DID YOU (NOT) LIKE ABOUT YOUR LAST JOB?

Interviewers seem to have trick questions on reserve, right? Rather than focusing on the negative aspects of the last company or manager you worked for, this is a great opportunity to expand on your career goals.

If your previous role had the makings of a "dead-end" job, then express your desire for more opportunities for advancement. Describe how important career development is to you.

You could also point out that you haven't been able to take advantage of your strengths. If you are looking for a role that plays to your strengths and offers a challenge, let the interview know.

There is also something to say about culture fit. If you can identify that the work style or environment was negatively impacting your performance, say so. Interviewers want to see that you will commit to an employer but they will understand that you need the company to do its part to help you thrive.

## WHAT MAKES A BOSS (NOT) GREAT?

This was one of my personal favorites in an interview. I remember how excited I was the first time I was asked this question in an interview. No, I wasn't excited to rant about how horrible my previous boss (or two) had been. It was so refreshing to be asked what I value in management.

This can be tricky because the tendency is to focus on the negative. One of the most important interview tips you can hear is to keep the answers and conversation positive. Rather than focusing on what you didn't like about a boss, think on why that trait is negative and what a better alternative would be.

From my experience, I had a manager who didn't keep me informed of important changes to processes or general workplace activities. While I wanted to say that I had a boss who made me look bad and uninformed, I answered that I believe a good boss needs to communicate well with his staff. I said that I believe a successful team needs to be informed and knowledgeable of changes through weekly meetings, frequent emails, or mentoring.

This answer indirectly states the negative traits of a "bad boss" while directly recommending a solution to the problem rather than focusing on the problem.

## HOW DO YOU HANDLE STRESS?

Stress is a part, even in small ways, of every role. Stress is also another negative topic that you can discuss with a positive attitude. There are two great tactics to answering this question.

You could highlight your strengths in task management, time management, organization, or teamwork and how they relate to how you handle stress. Whatever you do, do not say you have great "multi-tasking" skills. This term implies that you have a problem focusing and may stretch yourself too thin to be effective. If an interviewer uses this term, acknowledge that you prefer "task management."

The other tactic needs to be done carefully. Describe how stress motivates you and give specific examples of your work ethic. The basic answer, "Stress motivates me," is overused and completely ineffective on its own. Reinforce it with your positive attitude, ambition, and successful record of meeting goals.

## DESCRIBE A TIME WHEN...

Behavioral interviews and interview questions will present scenarios and ask you to describe how you would handle the situation. We will give you a few examples.

When an interviewer asks you to describe a time when you had to handle a difficult situation, make sure you describe the circumstances that caused the situation as well as how your actions produced a positive outcome. By using storytelling tactics, such as cause and effect, you will show employers that you not only can assess situations but apply your skills appropriately to solve problems.

An interviewer may also ask you to describe a time when you made a mistake and how you handled it. Answer honestly that you owned up to your mistake and took actions to correct the situation.

## WHERE DO YOU SEE YOURSELF
## IN FIVE YEARS?

There a few ways to approach this question. You could identify your long term goals, describe your ideal position, or define success from your perspective.

Interviewers will catch on if you are not excited about the position. They may not be looking for a candidate who considers this the "dream job," but they are looking for a candidate who will thrive in the role. If this is just a stepping stone toward your goal, then describe how this position will fit into your plans.

If your goals are to fill a management role and this interview is for a support position, show your ambition. If this role matches your ideal environment and you just want a desk where you can do your work in solitude, speak up. Describing your ideal position and how this role will help you gain the skills and experience you need to achieve your ideal position is a solid strategy.

Lastly, you could define what success means to you. If success looks like an office with a view, a team to lead, and awards for your sales achievements, then specifically identify how you plan to achieve these goals and attain success.

## WHAT ARE YOUR SALARY REQUIREMENTS?

When asked about your salary requirements, you need to have a fair expectation as well as a factual average in mind for your career level and industry. It's easy to offer a low number to try and underbid other candidates, but you need to be satisfied with the salary you requested if you receive the job.

Before attending the interview, you should have researched the job title and responsibilities in addition to the industry standards for compensation. Websites like Salary.com can be helpful in researching what is fair for your industry, your area, and your amount of experience.

You should also reflect on your own needs and background. Do not sell yourself short. An employer will pay you what they think you are worth; but if you don't recognize the value you offer, you will struggle to convince the interviewer that you are worth a higher salary. You also shouldn't accept a job offer with a salary that will not accommodate your lifestyle. It will not be worth the financial stress to come.

## DO YOU HAVE ANY QUESTIONS FOR ME?

There will be an opportunity at the end of your interview to ask any questions. The tendency may be to shake your head and get out of there as quickly as possible, but you shouldn't. Take this opportunity to ask vital questions about the company culture and expectations.

Ask how the interviewer would define success for this position and who previously held the position. This gives you a great idea about the expectations that management will have and if the position offers opportunity for advancement. Ask about a typical day for the role to also gauge expectations.

Ask about the company culture, specifically what the interviewer has enjoyed most about working at that company. This will put him or her on the spot to give some honest feedback about the company. Watch his or her body language carefully and listen to what they choose to focus on. If there is any hesitation, then this company may not be for you.

Before you leave, ask what the next steps are. This shows how interested you are in moving forward and puts you in control of the situation rather than waiting for the next move.

# CHAPTER 7

## EXPLAINING SPECIAL CIRCUMSTANCES

Interview questions are exhausting enough to prepare for, but you may need to prepare to explain certain red flags that appear on your resume. Overlapping dates, numerous short-term positions, and gaps in employment are all circumstances that an interviewer will be curious about.

While overlapping dates imply that you are exceptional at managing multiple priorities, it may concern an interviewer about your attention span. Did you get the second job because you were bored with your first job? How about your loyalty? Were you working for competing companies without even knowing it? You will want to ensure the interviewer that you are looking forward to new opportunities that will meet your needs financially as well as offer opportunities for growth.

# EXPLAINING NUMEROUS SHORT-TERM POSITIONS

Also known as job-hopping, having numerous short-term positions on your resume will send a few red flags to employers. Fortunately, there was something about your background that inspired the interviewer to consider you for the role and get to know you more. Be prepared to explain yourself.

The most common reasons for numerous short-term positions are related to school, health problems, family emergencies, new opportunities, and professional conflicts. I guarantee your reason is going to be less important than how you explain your reason. Employers understand that things happen, but you will want to keep the explanation light and positive.

If you have numerous short-term positions while you were in college, explain that you needed to find a position or company that would work around your schedule when your schedule changes. Your interviewer will keep in mind that you were pursuing higher education and that you were successful in managing your priorities at school while working.

Employers understand when health and family emergencies require you to make changes. Rather than focusing on the troubles keeping you from a steady job, draw the focus back to the skills you acquired over your entire career. Steer the conversation away from hardships appropriately. Try to keep your answers as positive and forward-thinking as possible.

*"Steer the conversation away from hardships appropriately. Try to keep your answers as positive and forward-thinking as possible."*

An ideal answer to why you have numerous short-term positions on your resume will express your desire to advance in your career. If you point out that you left a company (or two) because you were offered an opportunity for more professional growth, you present yourself as an ambitious professional looking for more responsibilities.

Even if you left a company (or two) because of conflicts with coworkers or management, the best approach you should take is to explain that the role or company wasn't a good fit. The most detail you should give should point back to the company culture not being a good fit for you or your career goals.

## EXPLAINING A LAYOFF

Gaps in employment can also be a red flag for employers. If you are asked to schedule an interview, you should expect questions as to why you don't have a consistent work history. One of the most difficult to explain are company layoffs.

The interviewer doesn't need to or want to hear about how you "got screwed" or how you weren't valued by the company. This is the opportunity to speak highly of your former employer and describe how well you handle change.

*"This is the opportunity to speak highly of your former employer and describe how well you handle change."*

Explain that the company restructured, downsized, or had a change in management because of the company's need for positive changes. Continue describing the positive actions you took next, such as taking online classes to improve certain skills or studying industry-related news and articles to stay up to date on trends and recent events.

## EXPLAINING GOING BACK TO SCHOOL

There are times where going back to school and working full-time are just not realistic. Taking time off work voluntarily to finish a degree that will open doors in your career is understandable and often admirable.

Explain to the interviewer that you value personal and professional development and that this time spent out of the workforce makes you more qualified for the role you are interviewing for. Interviewers will appreciate that this was a major decision that wasn't taken lightly and benefited your advancement.

## EXPLAINING FAMILY CARETAKING

Whether you took time off to be a stay-at-home parent or to care for an elderly or sick family member, employers will understand that your priorities had to change for a period of time.

You should describe any transferrable and related skills that you applied during your time caring for family. A few examples include time management, task management, child supervision, scheduling, appointment setting, etc. Make sure you have solid examples that reflect a professional interpretation of these skills.

## EXPLAINING YOUR RETURN FROM RETIREMENT

Sometimes a gap in employment can be a result of an unexpected end to your retirement. Many retirees are returning to the workforce. While those with a specialized skill set have an easier time standing out with over 20 years of experience, others may need to rely on other activities to stand out.

If you spent time during your retirement traveling or volunteering, you may have solid examples of transferrable experience that employers will consider. Showing how you stayed active and productive will certainly help your chances. For example, you may have improved your communication and organization skills without realizing it. If you spent your retirement not being productive, you may want to explore a few online classes or volunteer activities.

## EXPLAINING A CAREER CHANGE

Another scenario that may require an explanation during an interview involves candidates that are changing careers. Changing careers will require you to find ways to stand out especially when competing against candidates with more relevant experience.

During your interview, you will need to be able to explain how your skills are transferrable or how your qualifications make you the best match for the role. If you are a recent graduate with no relevant experience, you will need to rely on your education and the skills you acquired in class to qualify you.

*"You will need to be able to explain how your skills are transferrable or how your qualifications make you the best match for the role."*

When identifying transferrable skills, you will be challenged to think about your past experiences with a new perspective. For example, I worked with a client who had been a private tutor for over 20 years. She was looking to change careers as a business consultant or project manager. Her tutoring experience could be translated into consulting experience, and the other skills gained during her business ownership translated into project management skills and business acumen.

Did she consider these experiences transferrable? Not at first. After assessing her background with a professional, she realized that she had the skills for a role she was pursuing without 10+ years of experience working for a corporation.

## EXPLAINING SELF-EMPLOYMENT

Freelancing and self-employment is on the rise. The percentage of moonlighters, entrepreneurs, and new small business owners is rapidly climbing, which is causing employers some concern about the manageability and loyalty of certain candidates. Explaining your self-employment will require some careful consideration.

You can avoid presenting such blatant red flags by listing your company name and a descriptive title rather than "Owner" or "Founder." If you didn't operate under a DBA ("doing business as" name), you may want to consider listing the experience under a career note on your resume with a brief description of any related skills.

During the interview, try to downplay your self-employment. Yes, your business is a major accomplishment! Focus on any major accomplishments and how this new role fits with your career goals. The key is instilling confidence in your loyalty by focusing on the future.

# CHAPTER 8

## FOLLOWING UP

I've had several clients ask if Off The Clock Resumes provides Thank You Letter writing services. We don't, and we never will. Why? No hiring manager or employer will ever respond positively to a scripted thank you letter.

There may be nothing more impersonal and less genuine than a paid-for thank you note. It's easy to identify a generic template. This is your reputation and future we're talking about!

## THE MIXED SIGNALS

I recently saw a post on Facebook that a friend had engaged with. The photo was a conversation about following up after an interview and different responses from employers. Some consider it annoying and desperate to call back on a job. Then there are others that won't consider you unless you follow up.

Each interview, interaction, and conversation will be judged differently by each employer. Regardless of the mixed signals, it is best practice to take risks to present yourself in a positive light.

*"Regardless of the mixed signals, it is best practice to take risks to present yourself in a positive light."*

## BEFORE YOU LEAVE THE BUILDING

After your interview, make sure you get a business card for each person you interviewed with. There are several benefits to grabbing a business card. The biggest advantage is extending your professional network. The second advantage is giving yourself options for following up.

## SEND A CONNECTION REQUEST

Unless you are interviewing for a job at a family-owned business or in a small town, there is a good chance your interviewer is on LinkedIn. You will be able to use his or her full name or email address to find the right LinkedIn profile.

Sending a connection request on LinkedIn is personal without being desperate especially if you send a Personalized Invitation. You only have 300 characters to work with, so keep your message short and sweet. It doesn't take much to thank the interviewer for taking the time to meet with you and for considering you for the position.

This is also a great opportunity to stand out and make a bold, but certainly not desperate, move. Ask him or her to review your profile and provide a little feedback. Ask if there is anything you could add or improve based on what he or she may have learned about you during the interview.

This tactic is the best way to inspire a response. Your interviewer may recommend adding another skill that he or she may want to endorse after your interview.

After receiving a response and perhaps a new connection, return the favor. Endorse him or her for interviewing skills.

## A HANDWRITTEN CARD

If your interviewer or you are not on LinkedIn, send or deliver a handwritten thank you card. Use the company address on the business card to address the card if you are mailing it.

You could certainly send a brief thank-you email, but it's a little risky. Corporate email addresses are typically for internal use. Receiving an unsolicited email from an unknown email address may not be received or appreciated. Your message may be marked as SPAM or Junk. You could risk getting the interviewer in trouble for receiving non-work related emails to that address as well.

Your note should be brief and thank him or her for the time and consideration. Rather than asking for feedback, take the opportunity to make a lasting impression. You could identify why this particular opportunity aligns with your career goals or remind the interviewer why you are most excited about this position or working for this particular company.

Another great tactic is to comment on something non-work related that was said during the interview. Making a personal connection with the interviewer is a great way to stand out.

*"Making a personal connection with the interviewer is a great way to stand out."*

## A GLASSDOOR REVIEW

You can also leave a review on Glassdoor, a website where employees and job seekers can anonymously review companies and their management. While reviews are anonymous, you can mention your interviewer's name and mention something specific about your interview to make it easier to identify that you wrote the review.

To write a review, search for the company and find the Interviews section. Click the Add Interview button and complete the form. Take advantage of the "Describe the Interview Process" field.

You could mention how great it was to meet with your interviewer by name. Briefly identify something specific and positive about the interview.

*"Briefly identify something specific and positive about the interview."*

Here's an example: "My interview with Jessica went so well! She challenged me to think more about my long-term career goals and asked for specific examples of how I applied my skills in previous positions. She also gave me excellent feedback on my resume, specifically that she loved that I wore a tie that matched the color used for my name and section headings on my resume."

While it may seem silly, giving your interviewer some feedback will not only reflect well on him or her with management but reflect positively on the company for having a great review. Your review may inspire more job seekers to apply for openings which is helpful for recruiters. Your review may also provoke more positive feedback from others who had interviewed or worked at the company.

# CONCLUSION

## MORE TIPS

While this book is not a complete and ultimate guide to conquering job interviews, my hope is that the book has helped you prepare more for your next interview. Every company is different. Every interviewer will have his or her quirks, tactics, favorite questions, and goals. You shouldn't stress about pleasing every interviewer.

Instead, take these recommendations and use them to boost your confidence. If you already secured an interview, you have already convinced the interviewer that you are worth their time. The interview is just a meeting to make introductions and seal the deal.

If your interview doesn't go as well as you had hoped and you don't receive a job offer, take it as a sign that the company was not going to be a good fit for you and a new and better job is right around the corner. Never take an unsuccessful interview as a sign that you are not valuable or that you are a failure.

I want to wrap up the book with a list of our top interview tips in hopes that they will further encourage you.

## ANOTHER 30+ INTERVIEW TIPS

1.  Be passionate about the job opportunity.

2.  Describe how the opportunity will give you satisfaction.

3.  Give detailed examples that highlight your expertise.

4.  Don't make assumptions about the employer or opportunity; instead, ask lots of questions.

5.  Share your success stories.

6.  Buy a new interview outfit to boost your confidence.

7.  Show up with a portfolio or collection of your work including copies of your resume, your cover letter, letters of recommendation, and any articles you've written or performance reports.

8.  Discuss your problem solving skills with solid examples from your background.

9.  Don't forget to point out your computer skills.

10. Focus on your goals and the future

11. Show an interest in workshops, seminars, and other opportunities for improvement.

12. Practice your interview skills with a friend or colleague.

13. Be honest about being overqualified, if asked.

14. Stay positive and enthusiastic.

15. Do lots of research on the company before the interview using LinkedIn, Glassdoor, and other credible online sources.

16. Have energy and let your personality shine through.

17. Stay up to date on industry news and terminology.

18. Show motivation besides salary.

19. Don't only focus on job-related skills and point out your transferrable skills too.

20. Answer questions thoughtfully.

21. Take your time answering questions.

22. Take a deep breath and don't talk too quickly.

23. Ask questions about company culture and working for the company.

24. Have a firm handshake.

25. Do not criticize past employers or managers.

26. Show employers that you can be cross-trained.

27. Send a thank you gesture after the interview.

28. Ask for feedback about your interview before you leave.

29. Always direct the conversation toward job performance.

30. Discuss your strengths in detail.

31. Don't show up too early or late.

## STRUGGLING TO GET THE CALL BACKS
## YOU DESERVE?

## GET FREE FEEDBACK ON YOUR RESUME

Our Certified Professional Resume Writers will evaluate your digital formatting, visual presentation, and resume content to make sure that your resume is optimized for the modern job search.

**Upload your resume today:**

www.offtheclockresumes.com/free-resume-critique